9x5/04

THE THIRTEEN HOURS OF
HALLOWEEN

Dian Curtis Regan

Illustrated by Lieve Baeten

ALBERT WHITMAN & COMPANY • MORTON GROVE, ILLINOIS

Text copyright © 1993 by Dian Curtis Regan.
Illustrations copyright © 1993 by Lieve Baeten.
Published in 1993 by Albert Whitman & Company,
6340 Oakton Street, Morton Grove, Illinois 60053-2723.
Published simultaneously in Canada
by General Publishing, Limited, Toronto.
Printed in the United States of America.
10 9 8 7 6 5 4 3 2 1

The text of this book is set in Quorum Medium.
The illustrations are rendered in watercolor and pencil.
Design by Karen Johnson Campbell.

Library of Congress Cataloging-in-Publication Data
Regan, Dian Curtis.
    The thirteen hours of Halloween/Dian Curtis Regan;
illustrated by Lieve Baeten.
        p.   cm.
    Summary: A Halloween adaptation of the traditional
song "The Twelve Days of Christmas," presenting an
increasing number of pumpkins, bats, ghosts, and other
emblems of the season.
    ISBN 0-8075-7876-2
    1. Children's songs—Texts. [1. Twelve days of Christmas
(English folk song)—Adaptations. 2. Halloween—Songs
and music. 3. Songs.] I. Baeten, Lieve, ill. II. Title.
PZ7.R25854Th   1993   92-41207
                                                  CIP
                                                  AC

For Ashley and Michelle Regan. D.C.R.
For Wietse and Kobie. L.B.

In the first hour of Halloween, my best friend gave to me

a vulture in a dead tree.

In the second hour of Halloween, my mother gave to me

two pumpkins carved,

and a vulture in a dead tree.

In the third hour of Halloween, my father gave to me

three fat bats,

two pumpkins carved,

and a vulture in a dead tree.

In the fourth hour of Halloween, my sister gave to me

four witches' cats,

three fat bats,

two pumpkins carved,

and a vulture in a dead tree.

In the fifth hour of Halloween, my brother gave to me

five gha-a-a-a-s-tly ghosts,

four witches' cats,

three fat bats,

two pumpkins carved,

and a vulture in a dead tree.

In the sixth hour of Halloween, my cousin gave to me

six zombies staring,

five gha-a-a-a-s-tly ghosts,

four witches' cats,

three fat bats,

two pumpkins carved,

and a vulture in a dead tree.

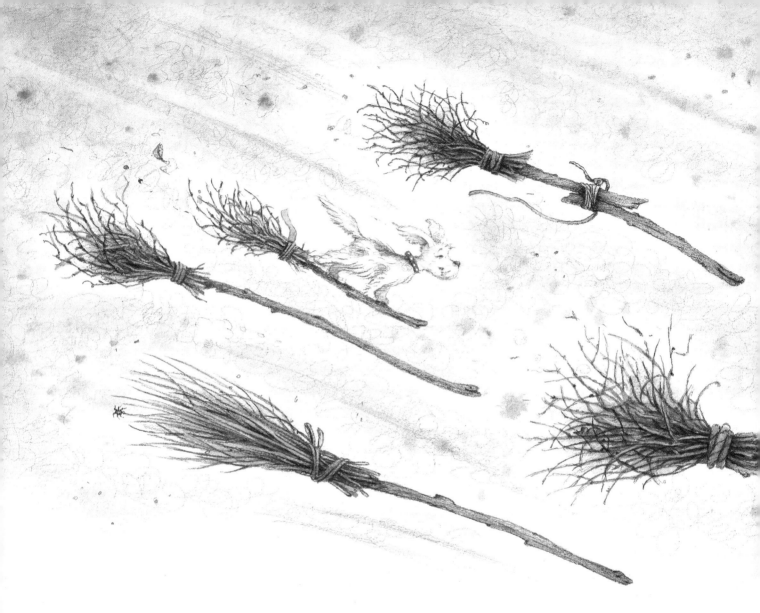

In the seventh hour of Halloween, my uncle gave to me

seven broomsticks flying,

six zombies staring,

five gha-a-a-a-s-tly ghosts,

four witches' cats,

three fat bats,

two pumpkins carved,

and a vulture in a dead tree.

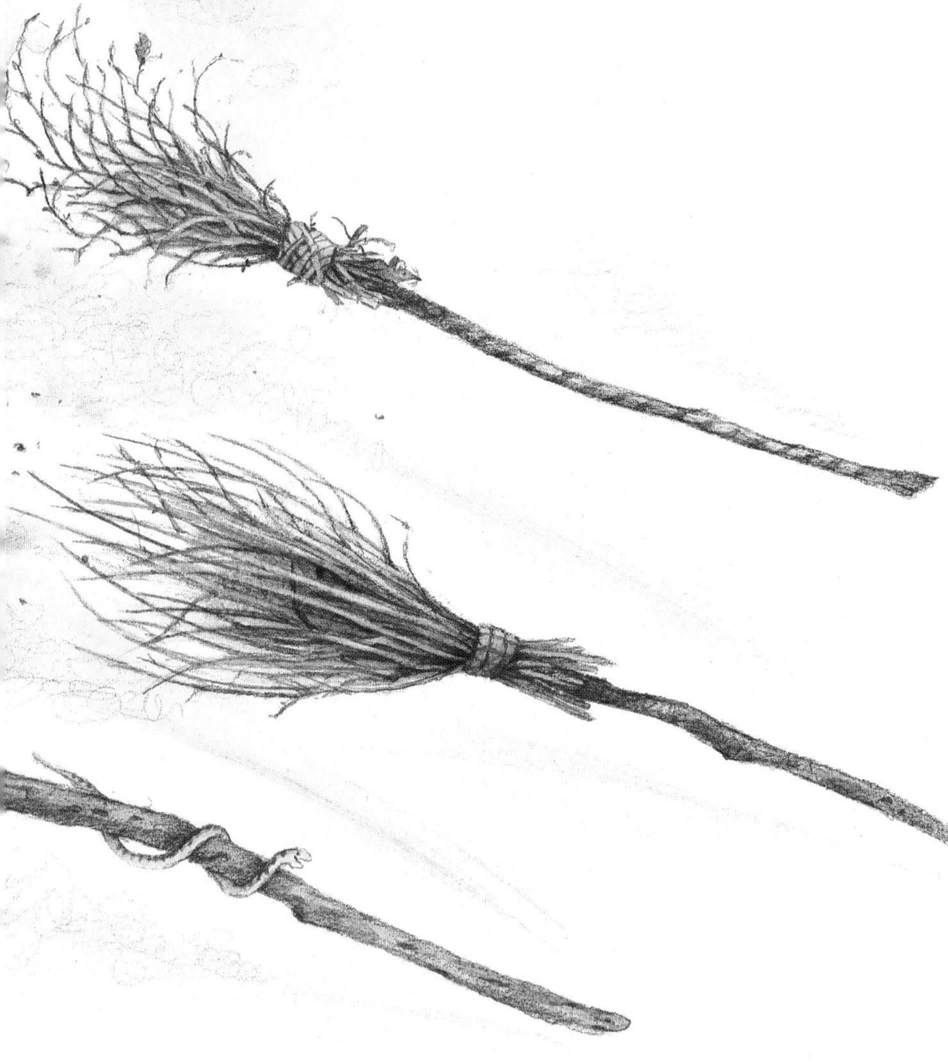

In the eighth hour of Halloween, my auntie gave to me

eight goblins grinning,

seven broomsticks flying,

six zombies staring,

five gha-a-a-a-s-tly ghosts,

four witches' cats,

three fat bats,

two pumpkins carved,

and a vulture in a dead tree.

In the ninth hour of Halloween, my neighbor gave to me

nine cauldrons bubbling,

eight goblins grinning,

seven broomsticks flying,

six zombies staring,

five gha-a-a-a-s-tly ghosts,

four witches' cats,

three fat bats,

two pumpkins carved,

and a vulture in a dead tree.

In the tenth hour of Halloween, my grandma gave to me

ten werewolves howling,

nine cauldrons bubbling,

eight goblins grinning,

seven broomsticks flying,

six zombies staring,

five gha-a-a-a-s-tly ghosts,

four witches' cats,

three fat bats,

two pumpkins carved,

and a vulture in a dead tree.

In the eleventh hour of Halloween, my grandpa gave to me

eleven mummies rapping,

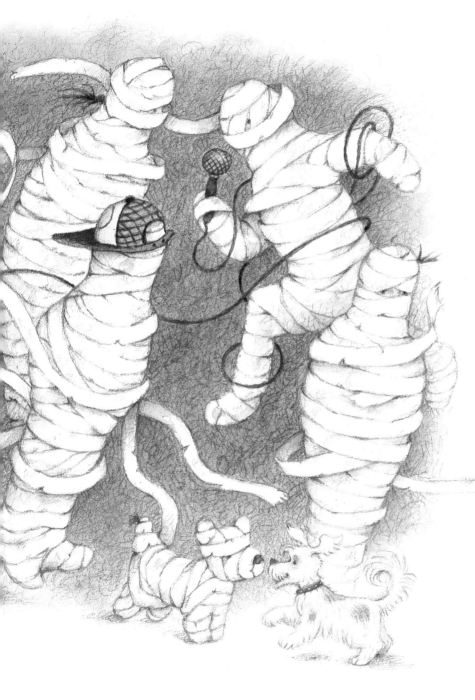

ten werewolves howling,

nine cauldrons bubbling,

eight goblins grinning,

seven broomsticks flying,

six zombies staring,

five gha-a-a-a-s-tly ghosts,

four witches' cats,

three fat bats,

two pumpkins carved,

and a vulture in a dead tree.

In the twelfth hour of Halloween, my teacher gave to me

twelve witches cackling,

eleven mummies rapping,

ten werewolves howling,

nine cauldrons bubbling,

eight goblins grinning,

seven broomsticks flying,

six zombies staring,

five gha-a-a-a-s-tly ghosts,

four witches' cats,

three fat bats,

two pumpkins carved,

and a vulture in a dead tree.

In the thirteenth hour of Halloween, I couldn't stand the noise,

so I gave away my creepy gifts.

Mother wanted witches,

Father took the mummies,

Sister wished for werewolves,

Brother hauled the cauldrons,

Cousin grabbed the goblins,

Neighbor begged for broomsticks,

Uncle hired the zombies,

Auntie l-o-o-o-o-ved the ghosts,

Grandma needed cats,

Grandpa, bats,

Teacher, pumpkins carved...

...but I kept the vulture in the dead tree!